Loading
the Airplane

Lesley Pether

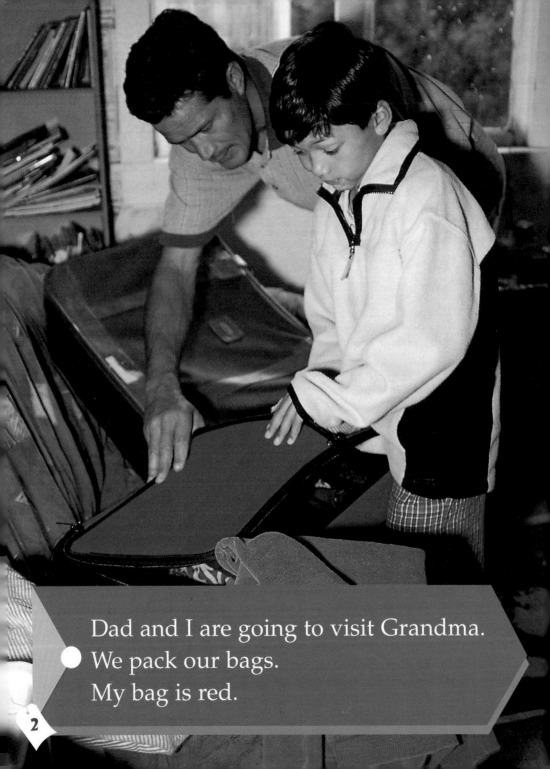

Dad and I are going to visit Grandma.
We pack our bags.
My bag is red.

Dad and I go to the airport.
We take our bags.

We show our tickets at the desk.
Tags are put on our bags.
The tags show where the bags are going.

FLORIDA

The bags are put on a conveyor belt.
They will be loaded on the airplane.

5

The bags are loaded onto a cart.
There are lots of different bags.

A truck pulls the cart to the airplane.
The airplane is waiting to be loaded.
Can you see my red bag?

The bags are loaded on the airplane.
Then the plane is ready to go.

9

When we land, the bags are unloaded. They are loaded onto a cart.

A truck pulls the cart inside.

Here come all the bags.
Can you see my bag?